WHALE ARIA | POEMS | RAJIV MOHABIR

ALSO BY RAJIV MOHABIR

POETRY

The Taxidermist's Cut

The Cowherd's Son

Cutlish

NONFICTION

Antiman: A Hybrid Memoir

TRANSLATION

I Even Regret Night: Holi Songs of Demerara

whale.
aria

POEMS | RAJIV MOHABIR

FOUR WAY BOOKS
TRIBECA

Library of Congress Cataloging-in-Publication Data
Names: Mohabir, Rajiv, author.
Title: Whale aria / Rajiv Mohabir.
Identifiers: LCCN 2023004567 (print) | LCCN 2023004568 (ebook) | ISBN
   9781954245686 (trade paperback) | ISBN 9781954245693 (ebook)
Subjects: LCSH: Whales--Poetry. | LCGFT: Poetry.
Classification: LCC PS3613.O376 W53 2023 (print) | LCC PS3613.O376
   (ebook) | DDC 811/.6--dc23/eng/20230206
LC record available at https://lccn.loc.gov/2023004567
LC ebook record available at https://lccn.loc.gov/2023004568

This book is manufactured in the United States of America and printed on
acid-free paper.

Four Way Books is a not-for-profit literary press. We are grateful for the assistance
we receive from individual donors, public arts agencies, and private foundations
including the NEA, NEA Cares, Literary Arts Emergency Fund, and the
New York State Council on the Arts, a state agency.

We are a proud member of the Community of Literary Magazines and Presses.

for Jordan Andrew Miles

CONTENTS

WHALE ARIA | POEMS | RAJIV MOHABIR

DOMINION

And God said, Let us make man in our image, after our likeness: and let them have dominion over the fish of the sea, and over the fowl of the air, and over the cattle, and over all the earth, and over every creeping thing that creepeth upon the earth.
—Genesis 1:26

Let there be light
skins and colored
skins. One to rule

the other.
A mandrake quickens
into greed-grab,

tears a page
from Genesis. Clods
of earth are clods

of God. Clods of earth
are clods of dendrites with dirt
skirting the ribs.

Memory of the untouched
is the more beautiful object.

From the streets
gashed bodies lament
this justice, burn-scarred

lives owned by light.

I strike a candle
against ruin, against

the separation of day

and night.

BOY WITH BALEEN FOR TEETH

My father wished
           to cast me back-
wards caste and all:
           a wrong catch,
saffron amniotic
           dripping off my black
whalebone gown.

My baleen burst through
pursed lips. When I smiled

Sunday's Lutherans gasped
then laughed-off horror,

He will outgrow it.
I opened my jaws

and sucked the plank-
ton from their eyes.

My father's pliers gripped
                my plates and he etched
the story of the son he wanted

onto my keratin. I gouged out
                his letters and into the channels
smeared India ink and plunged,

a fallen star into the abyss.

Deep silence swallows
the body. What
a fool I was,

        drawn to any
        glimmer. A whaler
        tore my dress

then stuck me
with his iron
after we kissed

        in a haze of chanteys
        and Cutty Sark.
        I want

to taste any
body that shines
in the dark.

Thunder pulsed from the clouds
in nested song and I was rain too,

starved for seasons, breaching
at dusk: a silhouette

on a darker sea—
for seasons I was faceless

trying to swallow constellations,
to roll a star-map on my tongue.

Once when lunging
          into the moon, the sea
showed me my face
          as I trembled midair.
Stars shone through
          the holes of my body.

IMMIGRANT ARIA

there they blow, there they blow, hot wild white breath out of the sea!
—D. H. Lawrence, "Whales Weep Not!"

To swallow new names like krill, dive.
    You have few tides before you
return to motion. Once this shrine

    was the abyssal plain. Once Empire
shackled you. Once you answered
    to monster, to dragon, spewing steam, fire

bellowing in the furnace of your hide,
    a migrant captured for brown skin's
labor. Somewhere inside the darkness

    where brews flame, a spirit hovers
over the deep. Once before Adam named
    you *illegal* you snaked, breaking

into air. Spit out his poison, jaw-clap
    the swell. With your aft-fin's trailing edge
churn surface to milk. In the beginning,

    you were formed with great light.

WHALE STORY

I. Matsya

And having sat thusly, I will guide you across the oceans.

—Vishnu in *Krishna* by Ramanand Sagar

Don't pack grains for this voyage.
        Pack folksongs. If you capsize
your lungs will seize up,
                catch fire of salt and sputter.

It's not my fault demons
        steal Vedas from your mouth
as you sleep. If you forget
                your prayers will you float?

Breathing air, I come
        to point out Manu's escape.
All about you, drowned
                men's arms reach up

to grab you, to drag you, to
        beg you to cool their hunger-
whitened tongues. Their fired
                iron and steel hooks,

will scald your hide
        wrought of undying sun.
One day your children
                will crack coconuts,

grind chutney from the tropics'

      plankton bloom, and beckon

demons to their gold.

             Tie your vessel to my horn

and offer garlands

      to Varuna, your own name

a mantra to the god

           of exile, the ruler of life.

II. Cetus

Andromeda,
you hallucinate awaiting
the beast
that swims to devour
you. The cetacean's
storm-eye withstands
the pressure of diving
nose first into the abyss.
Because pride chains
the innocent to rocks
for sacrifice, even if
you survive betrayal
by your mother
to the sea-god, how
could you possibly return
home? Your patria
will strip away your kith,
puncture your eye
should you dive,
bound as you are
for the tryworks.
Or perhaps a savior,
fair like chalk, will smite
the whale into mere
phantasm. You are obsessed
with reentering the womb
once it spits you out.

III. Bake-kujira

O phantom in calcium,
queer apparition
picked to the ghost—

O wraith-god of bone,
is it due to micro-
plastic, the hunt, or radiation

that you rise up
from the grave,
to unsettle rivers and tide,

harrowing and intent
to prophesy? Fish and
birds, warped and

misshapen, attend you.
Plastic gouges their guts—
rotting as Midway albatross

drying conjoined
as grey whales in Baja.

Every living intestine fills
with radioactive nuclides.

O Kujira, forgive me.
Forgive me

my toothbrush.

IV. Leviathan

> *Canst thou fill his skin with barbed irons?*
> *Or his head with fish spears?*
> —Job 41:7

O God of Abraham, Isaac, of Jacob,
     I have piked this monster
through the nose, lassoed its tongue
with rope, and carved its flesh
into Bible shape.

     I've seen the main transform
from coral to crimson, gallons
and galleons of gore frothing
in harpoon and fluke thrash;
the final sputter of hellfire.
You crush mighty heads
with one blink.

O God of eternal resource,
     I am your servant.
Your name be praised
as the walls of Jericho
tumble into dust.

V. Palaoa

Hanau ka Palaoa noho i kai
Born is the whale living in the sea.
—Kumulipo

So sit proudly in your museum room
your people will come for you soon.
—Brandy Nālani McDougall, "Lei Niho Palaoa"

Who controls the palaoa
carved into a tongue
and strung about their neck
with braids of human hair
is true aliʻi—a ruler who
controls the corpses
of beached whales. They possess
the tooth-ivory, this kinolau,
this carved palaoa, one bodily
form of Kanaloa, giving strength
to speech, tidal force to decree.
Yet today stolen and stashed
niho lei palaoa remain
behind museum glass
as American sonar pulses out.
The navy drives melon-headed
whales to scrape tonnage
against fringe reef, bleeding
from ears, to wither
on the *most beautiful*
beach the world over.
I shuffle my feet in Waikīkī's
gold, my skin roasting

its greed. A bleached coral
bites my heel. Whose place
have I taken—

Against wave-crash, singing
one song, tropic birds
and pigeons without breath,
now white now kea.

VI. Yunus

Then the fish swallowed him, while he was blameworthy.
—Al-Qur'an 37: 142

Nothingness thrummed within,
may God be merciful,

a djin in the heart of the whale.
I begged the seamen, *Heft this body;*

hurl me overboard. My prayer
a cord of light. But first

I must atone; stomach acid must
scald. I must come

to face dusk, swallowed whole.
I must write the poem

where I admit running away
with the neighbor boy, packing

a bottle of gin and condoms.
I must admit my failures as a son:

I left my father alone,
without an heir; I never used

the condoms. I break my name
in two, *-maha -bir*, holding

onto *bir*, the part that means *semen.*

BOY-NOT-BOY

At first there was only darkness wrapped in darkness.
All this was only unillumined water.
That One which came to be, enclosed in nothing,
arose at last, born of the power of heat.
—Rig Veda 10:129:3

As a child I lamented, *Drink from this*
       cup, stitch-rip sequins and tear your
petticoat. Carmine sari pleats into

       my brief's elastic I hid, which twanged
and burst, strung too tight. What color
       sing broken strings? My whale mer-

tail stuck my throat, a tussah delight too
       leviathan to hide. Now my dagger-
eyes, lined in moon-cured kohl,

       hurricane their bathypelagic coal. Hear
my gourd croon and sigh; my tune
       its own Veda. In the beginning, desire

descended to an earth bathed in night.
       Seeking sun, I leap from aphotic zone
to bring to the surface light; my hymn,

       a forgiveness to rise from fluke to breach.

HUMPBACK VOCALIZATIONS

In their North Pacific wintering waters, humpbacks sing the same, slowly evolving song. Learning strains from one another, they sing across the fathoms, their phrases and themes shifting in a pattern of small changes until they stitch new songs of older material.

Songs at the end of the summer transform from the beginning of the season. Biologists Hal Whitehead and Luke Rendell write that, in Hawaiian waters, groups of the North Pacific variety *alter their own songs in response to songs they have heard from other, very distant, humpbacks.*

This suggests music carries across thousands of miles. When apart, the songs of different socializing groups evolve at similar rates. Or at some meeting place mid-migration do humpbacks gather?

INVOCATION

Listen. You will hear my strain's
       echo ripple across the bay's sandy breast,
across the plains of Sargasso.

       A faint breeze will cause the maroon
kestrel of your breath to crest
       coral face. The Hunter-moon,

new and my spout, a lone grave mast:
       a salt plume, a meteor that wings
and flames into dusk. Blue's deep

       drips slow, below the surface to blur
the what's mine into you and fills
       us with wine. Come. Drink me

too. Sew my contours of phrase
       into a hymn to Manu, a hymn to Maui,
into whale dark aria fire-streak.

       We are stars bound into one psalm.

My ghost's a matelot, calling station
seamen—featureless windy
gales me home to kin. I make

gaunt sex of birch. In lullaby
askos poured rum full
from India, this and spreading

my Coolie re-veined. I now Kabbah
and Ayodhya staying me
into sea. Hair here heart,

ache, you will Creole
with long lilt, cut in half, brother. Stay,
refashioned. A fluke is a good

mistake, a kindness to others
in nets of melody, not parti
pris but evoking in you rapsi

to a new center, where you spit.

Mysticetes do not have phonic lips

                    or a *museau de singe* as with

whales like odontocetes

                    Larynges large as British call boxes

emit frequencies

                    Megaptera novaeangliae's U-

folds between upper and lower

                    respiratory systems vibrate

To hear sound, song, and noise
        alike, scientists must dig further
            into the biology of a humpback's
                bulla. They know it attaches
                    to the cetacean's jaw. The bulla looks
                        like a conch shell or a giant
                            clam that's been warped into a cave.
                                Or it looks like a sliced mushroom
                                    or the mouth of a cowrie shell,
                                but delicate. For sound to be realized
                            in the tympanic plate, fat and soft tissue
                        must vibrate against the jaw.
                    The cochlea joins to the periotic
                by a thin membranelike bone.
            This formation, the tympanoperiotic
        complex, processes sound
through bone conduction.

No one knows the why or where of it, but most agree whale song is moving. Why else send recordings in the *Voyager* spacecraft on the *Golden Record*? Is it the slow erasure of a species that wails out? Humans look for meaning and aesthetics in what they cannot understand—

Biologists Hal Whitehead and Luke Rendell wonder why whale song *rhymes* or is perceived as *rhyming as pattern repetition*. Is it lyrical? Is it cetacean rhetoric? How human language breaks apart at the point of conception. The echo is amniotic. We, once aquatic, heard as whales do.

Listen. You will hear my strains
        echo across the bay's sand
across the kelp and grass.

        Winding white pitches your bridle
to crimson, a crest to coral and iron
        searing faggots. Tonight morass

is niu sprinkles in gin, a mast
        of mezzo-soprano wishes
and flashes into dusk. Night's Qur'an

        drips slow, below the surf
to we two boatmen filled with
        wisecracks. Come. D'ua me

too. Sew my control and pick
        an icicle to Manu, an icicle to Maui,
into a constellation's fireside-stride.

        We are surahs bound into one air.

I am ghosted by Marine consternation
undersea waves of sound, merciless
to my kin. They make
skeletons of us bleach. In some myth
I was promised an odyssey
a never return home, not India
or any Navy blasting. I carry
pre-contact memory in my chest
sealed with coral. Turn your key here
Friend, you will be overcome
with squadrons, a queen dethroned. Stay.
Pretend. Your position's a fluke;
others drown in the loud sounds
scourging the deep, not melodious
but invoking your disappearance
as ears ruptured you dive too deep.

Megaptera novaeangliae's
tympanoperiotic complex is designed
to hear songs across great distances
at frequencies below what the human
ear can divine. It is a delicate
instrument of song and divination,
an environment under threat of shipping lanes,
seismic blasts, or naval sonar pulses. Songs
are made of notes, or base units humpbacks
emit at 20-4,000 hertz, in the range
of human hearing. Acoustic trauma
will rupture the process—
whales no longer able to hear one
another, not just a cultural loss—

In representations of the structure of humpback vocalizations, bioacousticians chart the anatomy of the line. Repetition, irregularity, looseness, and deft shifts of breath and phrase magic the water column.

aaa bcb cbc ded eff ded eff g

The rhyme sense in a complete song leaves the listener in a sonically unfamiliar place. In fact, the *g* cascades, a grand departure—a kind of sonic and poetic anticlosure asking for riff and response. Perhaps this is an eight-stanza poem, mediated through human interpretation of what we can only imagine, not living in a three-dimensional water column.

  O

According to cetacean biologists, a *unit* may be imagined tO be nOtes of humpback *song*.

| | | O | O | O |

A collection of *units* is called a *phrase* (Of up tO ten seconds). Modulated O frequency O

| | O | | | |

and amplitude the nOtes are wrOught into phrases humpbacks repeat into a *theme*. Whales,

| O   O   O | | | | |

which scientists postulate sing for aesthetics' sake (hence poetry), add *theme* to *theme*, they

| | | | | |

weave *songs* that last for up to twenty or thirty minutes each. Some, they repeat for days.

Litany my strains you hear; etch
   rip chords across the bay's cane beat
across the Sargasso stretch.

   Wind pitches the winger
and plunders your breech, breath,
    and whitecap. Tonight moonlight

Anubis and my sprat, a ghoul:
   a salutation comet plummets
and flamencos into dust. Night's drinkers

   slow and below the sugary surface
blur me and you and fill
    us with Madeira wine. Come. Uncork

my bota. Take my drops as words
   into a birdsong, a humansong
or a demigod meteorite light streak.

   We are many gods bound in one plan.

Dry spirits at market constitute
shaky legs pitch plastic into
reef guarded by Americans. I make

skeletal trim for Anthropocene myth
I was promised a humped back
instead trash bags pitched

into my sea village in strains. I cry
human shit storms fill my belly,
scrape my reef. Put your ear to my

pleats, Winged One, I am overcome,
my intestines cut in half. Stay.
Cut open my flute and throat folds,

a kindness for another drowning
in webs of netting, an alien
invocation of your vaps!

before binds and plastiglomerate.

Whale song constantly evolves though the extinction event looms—
That great god. Whales in the same regions sing similar, if not the same,
songs during the same times, each whale shifting tune and phrasing
to match what they hear.

When they return to Hawaiian waters they will pick up their song
where they stopped; the song they sing now is unique to this area.

What whales communicate

leaves scientists

and musicians speechless.

Do their songs dream sustainability,

urgency

in mating, feeding behavior,

play, competition,

poetry's gesture—

or

something yet undreamt?

Living my strains you hear
         etch rivalries across the bay's plastic,
across the stiches of sea grass.

         Trash bags pitched, my wingspan
pinched, indentured to sonar
         and pen caps. Tonight moored

to Anthropocene, my sprawl spooks:
         a Naval salute. My meter falls
and flames flam into dawn. Night,

         slow and below the sunrise,
I am you and you are me, despite
         the moon's cold light. Come.

Sew my manmade words as grains
         of mana, the strain aboard boats,
a constellation's salve. We are

         many bound in one plastiglomerate.

My spirit's marine, constant
in sea-legs—featureless when you
regard only my skin. I make

skeletal sense, beached. In my myth
I was promised a voyage back
home to an India, borders shifted,

my village renamed. I carry
home in ship-song sternum-deep,
fringed in reef. Put your ear to my chest,

dear heart, you will be overcome
with voyage cut in half. Stay.
Transform. You will grow a fluke and moan

kindly to the Others underwater
in webs of melody, not atavist
but evoking in you comeback

to the center, where you now spout.

UNDERWATER ACOUSTICS

Imagine the bluest electricity
of the coral sea. Dive headfirst from the bow,

your arms stretched out
before you in hallelujahs.

A mother and calf slap the surface
and you are caught
in the crossfire of calls.

All your organs quiver.

Once you immerse yourself in unending strains
the tones will haunt you:

ghosts spouting sohars you've called
since childhood. They breach

and crescendo inside the vessels
of your brine. How you long

to touch and to be so touched
by the dark giants under your skin.

Some songs breathe *you*.
Your body already knows.

In the evening ink, long
voices vibrate in your throat.

Open your mouth and spit.

WHALESONG

Silt fogs my eye's anemone.
        It's clear I can't see you. A bird sticks
my pipes, its feathers reach

        surgeon's fingers to trick-clown
my ventral pleats. Do you find a Mars
        heart ablaze inside my quick, a hazy

thing drowned in wine? Your arm
        so deep, it chokes my fist-sized throat.
I cut this song's mooring to sail

        for your ear, its acoustic birth fading,
dawn's dusky fate. What scintillates
        at start, sinks to fossil's lithic

stone. What once berthed your body
        sea-changed into hollow imprint
and at the far shore, alone,

        cries out in loss's slate froth.

GOLDEN RECORD

In the Gulf, I am a shadow, upside down,
singing to the coral. The water teems

with copepods and echoes.
I fear the night-terror of oil-rig drills,

blast-holes hollowing my ribs where folksongs
flourished. Of the erased, scientists

raise dioramas and copies in resin.
A pale record of the fifty-five languages

orbits from the space station, and on that plate,
whale song. From the gold disk, a copy,

a woman's voice asks, *jaat kahan ho akeli*—
Where do you go, alone—

I still perch on the cantering night horse;
my colony-body crumbles into fossil.

Even at home in Boston, no one understands
what I ask for when I say *birah*—

it has two definitions in English, one
is *warrior*, and the other: *loneliness*.

ANCESTOR

My language is petrified
like a Pliocene whalebone fossil
        though cane vestiges inside

my brine sugar me daily,
        though Hindi no longer lines
my tongue or accessory denticles.

        I feel deep tympani, not in hind
limbs, the calcium of sacral
        vertebrae, not the daggers of teeth,

nor the alembics of legacy.
        O Aji, the litany of your throat
on the SS Jura you stowed

        aboard, haunts. A head submerged
hums your wail and guides
        calves into breach. To bind you

        to my breast, I scrimshaw your
good name onto whale bone. I bear
        your sugar-scars like poems,

        score your femur into coil.

ORAL HISTORY

issa bole, *ungari hiya rakh le,*
hathan ke dekhke hamar khissa maan le

Marine biologists read rorqual keratin
as diaries. Just like tree rings, baleen

records mysteries of diet and thalassic
migration, the pocks of drought and plenty.

Continent-side, I've grown osteocytes
of oxygen, carbon, nitrogen, frayed on stories

of survival: the days Ma could afford chicken
for curry, the weeks we ate bare saltines.

Hunger bored into aubade, carved lyrics
into our bristles. Want naturalized its holes

in trabecular serenade. Dark. Hard. Worn.
Do we belong yet, abraded as America?

Jesus said, *Put your finger here*
Look at my hands and believe

CULTURAL REVOLUTION

In 1996, having become familiar with the song of the east Australian humpback, [Michael Noad] heard one whale singing a new and totally different song, with new phrases and themes. In 1997 this novel song took over; by the end of the season virtually all the humpbacks passing Peregian Beach were singing it.
—Whitehead and Rendell, *The Cultural Lives of Whales and Dolphins*

How pleading cries overleap oceans
         into rivers of sound scientists deem
non-human revolution, mystifies.

      A lone soloist lights the seaboard
in new tones, a sonic blaze to streak
        swells, to sew new chanteys before

he forges a life worth its poetry. His
        voice haunts night oceans in silver,
intoning dagger dialect though white

      faces insist, *Speak English, here; write*
"universal themes." My minor scales
        queer a nation; my hands teach

by drumbeat. I know you fear tongues
        like mine, what arias our spells knell.
Believe: in America Bhojpuri rises.

      aa sakha, hamar sang bhajan baja.

ORIENT ARIA

Whales swim about a million nautical miles during their lifetimes, navigating the seas by starlight.

—Aimee Nezhukumatathil, "Whale Song and Starlight: Making the Case for Wonder"

Ma's lullaby wove a zodiacal gleam
in my chest. Maps of mythic
heroes and fools etched in my once

Indian palms: Cetus the whale stars,
Sun, the sky-map, a net of meridians,
Jupiter and Saturn meet, conjunct

in the eleventh house. *You will travel
far, beta.* Water journey is my *yehi 'or,*
a home, a dowry-wealth, that bursts

into glister. To align with Polaris
I intone Ma's creation lullaby
looking up into the jet sky,

my voice steeped in Southern midnight;
my each sojourn jewels me in ruby.
Cetologists once believed humpbacks

to be astronomers, to return to where
forebearers taught arias, with precision,
to point their bodies like arrows,

guided by the song-shine of stars.

NATURAL AESTHETICS

It shouldn't surprise
that an animal's size
determines a voice's timbre
or that too much regard
for technique loses the image
that tricks presence
and absence, both honey-
dipped daggers. Speed up
a humpback song
and a nightingale calls
in rounds, in codas,
in fermatas and repeats.
Speed it up too much
and the rorqual disappears.
It took musician-scientists ages
to discover that whales
croon in patterns,
like humans do, in different
pace and pitch, learn songs line
by line, verse by verse, like
the Vedas or liturgy
I've memorized now lain
as sunbaked brick, still,
unmoving, unlike deep music's
liquid. What poetry
have I missed, missing the silk
for the worm, filling
my cetacean-cello chest
with the mud of naming; damning
with the noise of repetition.

INTERPRETING BEHAVIORS

bina jawab mile uu barah saal se awaaj dewe hai...
ki uu jane ki koi nahi sunal

Today scientists take interest in phenomena
that do not occur with even frequency.

For example: why doesn't the only other
desi fag on Oʻahu text after you harpoon

each other at Lēʻahi Park? Does his tail slap
mean to silence your calls when you say, *we're one species*?

You swallow a span of krill and upside down, sing
the Sindhi folksong he taught you: *When the British*

sailed what weakness did they leave? Does he mean
your connection was one-sided like Kimiko's whale

crooning at 52 Hz, the only of his kind
who can sing his poetry to you in Hindi?

> *For twelve years he's been calling out to no response...*
> *That it knew no others listened—*

SACRAMENT

My sister warns to choose either
        addiction to rum or to heartbreak
before I invite you up

        to sunny-side your eggs. But tonight
I flirt with angst. You turn my heart
        down like sheets drowned in brine.

You've already cut through and swim
        my arteries. I'm not sorry
for the blood storm's sorrow or how

        rain clouds seep into my thorax
and inundate me with phantom vows
        you swear you'll never. My temple

sinews do not bind bricks into a holy
        site worthy of Hajj nor Tirupati,
but a ballad that endures a nautical hour,

        where I break first then drink your trace.

ANATOMY LESSON

Where are the men which came in to thee this night? bring them out unto us, that we

may know them.

—Genesis 19:5

Megaptera novaeangliae means
      "big-winged New Englander," though the largest
was hooked in the Caribbean Sea. Whale
      mouthlines run high, though blowhole crests prevent

flooding between gasps. Diving into night's
      sky-mirror, they arch caudal peduncles.
Coupled with the prominence of a dorsal
      fin, whalers once called them "hump-backs."

A man devoted to his two-inch-deep
      walnut-sized center, can only enter
one kingdom that turns to salt the wayward.
      The Hebrew word *'Ămōrāh* means "deep" bend,

a hymn-gifting for "copious water," *to know,*
      as in to fuck, to prostrate before Provincetown.

VESTIGIAL BONES

jaunse tu bhagela ii toke nighalayi
je andar rahe uhi tohar jahaaj nast kari

The remnant of hind limbs puppets an origin
play that strings baleen to terrestrial

ancestors. Occasionally whales sport hind legs—
as in Vancouver in 1949,

a harpooned humpback bore eighteen inches
of femur breaching its body wall. Disconnected

from the spine, what is their function but to rend
the book of Genesis into two? Why regard

scripture and exegesis as legs and fluke,
sure to fall away, and not eat beef nor pork? Why

do I need Hindi in Hawai'i as a skeletal
structure, a myth to hook my leviathan jaw?

What you run from will swallow you,
what's inside will splinter your boat.

INSIDE THE BELLY

Noble and generous Cetacean, have you ever tasted Man?
—Rudyard Kipling, "How the Whale Got His Throat"

I

The seaman James Bartley screamed as he slid down a sperm whale's maw in 1891. He was in the stomach for fifteen hours, unconscious in the stench of digesting fish. He survived after his shipmates sliced the belly open and pulled his twitching body into bed, where he stayed for almost a month.

(If this happened today he would take a selfie.)

According to the Jonah-tales, he lost his sight and his skin whitened. He wasn't holding any blade.

II

A black-swallower can take a man twice as big as himself, his jaws distensible.

Catching them by the tail, he walks them over to his mouth.

This is the marine biology of deadly desire.

By most imperial standards in 1891, by the British East India Company, my biology is a metaphor.

I am dark skinned (for my family's *Indian*).

As a child I prayed to be white until my foreskin started to whiten.

This is not the deep, so spotting men is not impossible.

Cables crisscross the seafloor, a copper map.

The internet is a type of black-swallower too.

III

A humpback hums as it tongues me. He doesn't spit me out after I
come in his mouth. I want to shed my skin for a white coat. I ride
him into the starless cold water of the unnamed. His flanks toss me
from the bow, make the scales fall from my eyes.

IV

According to the Royal College of Surgeons, any mating is a death wish.

A wish for whiteness is every white man you bed.

Consider the bull shark that swallows a blowfish whole or why you
    refresh your screen with the "Load More Guys" feature on the app.

When it reaches the stomach it endures the acid and inflates before
    chewing through the shark's stomach lining.

Kipling's sailor placed a grating in the whale's pharynx to protect it from
    STIs but you like to cast cowries—stomach acid kills everything.

Your stomach still lurches with each tri-tone ring: which white man
    will you invite inside tonight, let erase you?

MUSEUM

Who opened the graveyard
door? A breeze scrimshaw-
scratches the halls.

Grey. Ash.

Cetacean
silhouettes soldered into snuff mulls
with silver lining.

On your bones
I draw me
stabbing

your lungs until you spit fire.

Should I hang
your milk-spit frame from rafters

for fathers to point out
beards and beer to adventure-eyed sons,
naked under death

etchings, stirred to plunder
by the leaf-rattle of a desecrated temple?

It's time
to staff the scarscore,

to cast new gods
of bone

and gore.

DISSECTING THE TAY WHALE

Oh! it was a most fearful and beautiful sight,
To see it lashing the water with its tail all its might
—William McGonagall, "The Famous Tay Whale"

You must first lance and kill
a whale to know it. Like John
      Struthers, the anatomist, cut open

the Tay Whale, to write his tome,
      naming the creature *Megaptera longimana*
before humpbacks were loved

      for their wings' charismatic top-side
slaps. Why must we slay the sea-
      beast to recognize its beauty?

A baleen-giant pierced from
      a whaleboat, a sailor splits its keratin
into corset ribs. Of the drink's plenty,

      what can I tell, empire's engine-
rev rolls coal: plumes of exhaust
      not spume. And if I trill of the beautiful,

is it already belly-up; words spun
      into a question, then image and cadence
of inquiry of what was once

      supple, now staid, now drying out?

CARCASS

That year alone five humpback calves washed up,
bodies precarious on the coral's razor edge.

Bellybuttons raw from birth, parents slap *farewell*.
But I make this human. Nani's mother's spine

screamed into motion aboard the ship
her mother died on. *Amma*, she would never say,

Tamil extinct on her tongue. At Kahuku Point
scientists bring to shore what vanishes:

a one-ton body dragged to Hale'iwa
corn-cobbed by tiger sharks. Do baby bones

reveal holes of their parents: calcium weakened
by diabetes, molasses, and rum? The scientists

trailed the deflated body behind boats for processing.
In Lusignan, Nani's mother cut her loose to tide.

BIRAH

Crests blow spouts that crash against
rock and asphalt. The sea yields
its salt as a wind howl or mist or

wraith. My windshield grays shades
of phantasm. You tumble in whale fall
as calcium stone. Beached, deadened

coral clouds the sand in whites and bleach.
On the stretch of shore, rose petals dry
at noon, perfume rising as tiny crowns,

curls of grave nostalgia: palmfuls
of whispered vespers cast to crystals.
So far from you, my petals

parch like this body's du'a.

DREAM

A hurricane strands a humpback
that croons from land, soon
to bloat in surf, unable to bear
the weight of meat, lungs gored
by rib. Beneath, copepods

and powdered mollusk shells
perform their diatom orchestra
in tiny voice, as salt packs them
tighter together. You utter
a spell of letters: *mysticetes*, and

corals sprout from your pharynx.
Clownfish scintillate in anemone
as if to say, *O eye, be drawn by*
the wild, fire-color you will be.
Your body opens into a coral reef,

triggerfish and wrasse play
amongst the polyps of your chest
until you roll back onto the beach
next to the other vertebraed creature.
Your voice carries its noise

to swirl in starlight long after
you shake into clay and teem
with microbial life. Burning
in the tryworks of blubber, ashore
in sun, helpless you voice too,

the fire-song that steams in air
as a shadow cry. One day you will
luminesce until you bleach into rock
dust. But now, you can do nothing
yourself except dissolve, *balaena*

beside you, melodious elsewhere,
but guttural here. Not *mystical*
ballerina a name masked in cognates;
you ask, *Balma, is this my voice or*
the rorqual's? Water, wave, grit of whelk

and conch, spin ballads in tumble
from afterlives, hiss in waves.
The orchestra erases, and fills
with motion divots of sand
where your whale body once lay.

GHOST ARIA

When no one's around I play gin
        with your wraith. Tarot me, Ouija me,
as if our hand is straight. How can

        I *Rummy!* you when all it takes
is a draw to keep a marooned heart from
        attack? Across the fringe reef I scrape

my knees and they don't heal for weeks.
        You are the penny scent of my blood. When
in the surf you submerge your ears

        what wail do you hear? I torture myself
into alpha state, dreaming your face
        painted in bar-light. Someone hands you

a flask and fingers your tie. You're a flush
        and discard. I turn up the silence.
I admit it's the full-stop period, that iris

        at the phrase's end that terrifies—

SOUND NAVIGATION AND RANGING

praise your capacity to smother

whales and fish and wash them ashore

to save them from our cruelty

——Craig Santos Perez, "Praise Song for Oceania"

I. Sonar

Have we forgotten how to speak to each other? You don't understand my words until they're blaring. Here is my universe. America, you map my cosmos to bomb it. You draw me and then I am no more. To you I can only have shape or life, never both. This is our new language, how we call out to destroy each other. By the time I describe the whale's beak, it's already something else. A beak is not a beak, but a sequence of locatable differences. Congratulations. You are stranded in your mid-frequency active sonar that curls poetry of salt ripples. Such a stunning dazzle, every living thing flees from its incisive craft. I don't want to be seen post-MFAS, resonance imaged, echo-range bombasted into bleeding eardrums. Noise. Noise. You speak an invented language as droplets of fire that wave and scorch from your craft intent to define and erase.

II. Jezebel Monster

Imagine you call out across the water and hear an answer. Fewer and
fewer of your kind migrate the old routes, being prey to plastic and
the US government. Yes, I said it. You are mostly alone and this is
a miracle. Or rather simulacra. A steel hull peopled with men who
jerk off together in their bunks, who press a button that emits a low
frequency in your dialect. Being so far from their partners they groan
from the shower. But I don't feel sorry about their self-induced exile
but sorrow at their imposed new tongue. Imagine the elation when
I hear my sister singing a Hindi song, its beat sampled. First the
British, now the Americans won: no one in my house speaks anything
but English. Is this appropriation or homage? A foreign or heritage
language? Some analysts think the pulse they hear in their vessels are
fin whales crying out in loneliness.

III. No Chocolate No Curry No Rice

Grindr is a geosocial network of fags across the forty-eight and then
some. In Brighton, I once mapped a man's pelvic floor before we
dredged or even smelled each other's breath. Don't call me a bear
even though hair feathers my shoulders. White is standard: Desi fags
are curry: "ethnics" are food items to be consumed. Who doesn't
eat it with rice or prefer chocolate mousse to vanilla? The ways to
keep me out of your club are too many I've started bouncing myself.
Once a man called me his chicken-tikka-masala though the dish was
actually invented by the British in London just like what we call India
or Guyana today. I know how to roast then grind masala. Go ahead,
tap my pic. My spermaceti will not go to waste by candlelight if
you're Navy, we're in Hawai'i, and it's fleet week.

IV. Controlled Exposure

A metal whale beneath the brine calls out to the blue whale and
disrupts feeding and displaces them in a net of a similar language,
an anthropogenic dialect designed to scald their eyes underwater
and destroy their ears. If they are not fluid and fluent, they perish.
Their own calls are masked and their speech community drowns
in a naval pulse. Let's experiment. Slowly baleen whales react to
simulations of mid-frequency sonar and the poison of missionized
radiation. My great grandmother wouldn't understand a word I say.
My grandmother heard *garbar-garbar* for *no species (humpback, grey, and fin
whales) show signs of recovery.* We've been exposed, changed our names to
enter universities.

V. RIMPAC: an Island with a Colonial Disorder Speaks

The rim of the Pacific was *terra*
nullius once upon a time. And now I

pack my rim as often as I can with naval
officers and enlists. But it's not

rape. I am ready tonight. Combat ready—
the Indo-Asia-Pacific fleet

ensures warfighting and *leads*
America's rebalance.

RIMPAC is our safe word.

It's just a game, relax. It's all empty
land, come and torpedo the coral, come

and reap the whales along the rivulets
and tributaries. Come, aggression

                    is healthy, is American.

VI. Mass Stranding

The US Navy pan-fries the seafloor with bursts of sonar at 235 decibels. National security burns melon-headed whales with gas-bubble lesions. They dive deep into the dark to flee a suddenly bright night. *We are safe. We are safe. The military secures us.* The pulse floods for hundreds of miles. Beaked Whales belly up. Many of us suffer bleeding in the brain. Such metallic blasts alter our diving patterns. Air bends into pockets. We float pelagic with large bubbles in our organs. Panic. Or do you feel the tidal pull of the ocean at your fins as you graze your body in the surf's wake. *We are safe. We are safe. The military secures us.* There's nowhere to run. Not up. Not down. Look at the hill from Kaʻena; see the satellites. How many brown people dry in the sun? Have you ever lost your own balance? *We are safe. We are safe. The military secures us.* Can you move? Who is crossing the kalapani for you?

BLOWHOLE

I trace your
passing on a skin mark, that
spot you left, a memento,

god-trance
of turned-up surf.

Your salt, a vesper whispered
through sooted nostrils,
a sooth said: *Fuck.*

Cunt. Yet
fecund. And come. Anoint

my hollow with just the tip.
A cross in coconut oil

on your fingers and spread
on my lips that crack like whips or
wisps of voice in scream

as I risk drowning.

My head a hydra,
prepare to empty over and

to be overrun.

PLASTIVORE

Humpbacks swallow six parts plastic for one part plankton.
—Stephen Collis

      Pick a pectoral peck of polycarbonate
particulates. Wreath the shoal
      in bubble nets, open your teeth.

Swallow polyvinylidene
      chlorides, polymides, poly-every-
kind of toothbrush to scrub

      baleen, and micro-dot hand wash.
Now heat a canticle cycle:
      soften, cool, harden. Look,

you splash in the kingdom
      genus species of plastic. After
bones dust, a polyethylene pile.

      What other remains endure?

STOMACH FULL OF TRASH

Put your hand inside
                     my wound. You stud me
         in jewels and now

I float in the bay.
                     With your arms submerged,
         pass my pharynx and reach

into my pouch of skin
                     folded on skin. Pull out
         the garbage in my gut,

gleaming as the razor jewels
                     of empire. Is my plastic
         a prophet sent to predict

your doom? The Coolie is here
                     to serve you. Here's the oil
         from my head that keeps me

afloat and bloating. Lay on this
                     palanquin of my ribs
         and baleen. I will carry

you on my back. I will dress you
                     in rhinestones and sequin
         scales and you can penetrate

my deep as a mermaid—
    half fish and all human
  desire for conquest.

COMEBACK

Returning to Bellingham Bay,
humpbacks lunge into krill
clouds. Cetacean resurgence stuns

August mackerel shoals, northern
blooms now at silver capacity.
Whalers once drove rorquals

to markets as lamp oil and umbrellas.
What is a body but to be rendered—

In 1907 five hundred white men
shook East Indians from prayer,

broke dholak drums, pushed out
who they called *Hindu Hordes*.

We are still being flensed
of papers, stripped to the quick
in public. And yet, in America's

thieved straits I sing dark-
bodied chutney. Listen,

the Salish Salt again hums.
Off Semiahmoo Bay, see a cow
teach her yearling to blow

a toroidal vortex. Despite
whale irons, ruin, despite
expulsion, *Get Out* scrawled

on our temple walls, we return.
To our summer qawwali-

kirtan, we return, while
flukes beat the drum-skin sea.

RETURN MIGRATION

You can't herring-net me. I'm red
          and you're gone. Time's fish-eye
tricks me to think you're bigger

          when I am underneath blowing you
bubble-rings to tickle your belly.
          Keep laughing. How can you dream

of any algae bloom or fuller rhumb?
          I fish-scale sparkle and scrape
your baleen and taste your song.

          To migrate. I flounder, a jester;
you torpedo, an outrigger. When you
          return why call or canoe out?

Ask the Pacific reef about nutrients.
          Beyond volcanic slopes the heart's
desert betrays silence. It's time.

SHIFT TO SILENCE

And it came to pass at the end of forty days, that Noah opened the window of the ark
which he had made; And he sent forth a raven, which went forth to and fro, until the
waters were dried up from off the earth.
—Genesis 8: 6-7

Our absence from shipping
lanes, our isolation zoom

of voice and face from
Ararat to Ararat peak,

means whales resume
their most ancient web,

stretching across the entire planet,
which means less measured

ambient, roving noise / as shipping slows and cruise / liners
     beach, a respite /

                      from the unrelenting drone
                      cetaceans strain above

                      from Alaska to Hawaiʻi;
                      from the Dominican Republic

                      to Boston; Baja to Washington,
                      to hear and be heard

in the new, old breadth
of silence. *This year signs are*

more encouraging though *more needs / to be done* against *oceanic smog, /* article
    after essay beseech. /

Our pandemic quiet lessens
whale stress. Spouts bloom

as ghost trees, broken
into tracheal bough, a healthy

grove during our quarantine,
our *forty days and nights'*

rain; seeding what grows
into an olive-twig.

WHY WHALES ARE BACK IN NEW YORK CITY

After a century, humpbacks migrate
again to Queens. They left
due to sewage and white froth

banking the shores from polychlorinated-
biphenyl-dumping into the Hudson
and winnowing menhaden schools.

But now grace, bodies of song
return. Go to the seaside—

Hold your breath. Submerge.
A black fluke silhouetted
against the Manhattan skyline.

Now ICE beats doors
down on Liberty Avenue
to deport. I sit alone on orange

A train seats, mouth sparkling
from Singh's Roti Shop, no matter how
white supremacy gathers

at the sidewalks, flows down
the streets, we still beat our drums
wild. Watch their false-god statues

prostrate to black and brown hands.
They won't keep us out
though they send us back.

Our songs will pierce the dark
fathoms. Behold the miracle:

what was once lost
now leaps before you.

NOTES

"Boy with Baleen for Teeth" is after a poem by Ansel Elkins. This poem was set to music by Michael Genese for mezzo-soprano, baritone, and piano.

"Boy-Not-Boy" and other poems in the tercets with alternating indentations are derived from the structure of humpback whale songs as delineated by: Mercado, Eduardo, et al., "Stereotypical Sound Patterns in Humpback Whale Songs: Usage and Function." *Aquatic Mammals*, vol. 29, no. 1, 2003, pp. 37–52, https://doi.org/10.1578/016754 203101024068.

"Humpback Vocalizations" shows how I've manipulated the following chart to come up with the poetic structure of the *whalesong poem*. It, too, is from: Mercado, Eduardo, et al., as cited in the Note above.

Humpback songs are constituted of units, phrases, and themes, and organized into songs and then into more complex song structures. I have parsed humpback song to use the component parts to form a poetic (and sometimes irregular) form. Humpback whale songs build on each segment and the assemblage of particular patterns.

According to the cetacean biologists a *unit* may be envisioned as the *notes* of the *song*. A collection of *units* is called a *phrase* (up to ten seconds); the *phrase* will be repeated into what is called a *theme*. It's a collection of *themes* that are known as *songs*, which will last up to thirty minutes each. *Units* of song I have interpreted to mean *syllables* (5-10 per line), *phrases* are *lines* (with a rhyme scheme; roughly ten syllables, though this is not exact, an irregularity that allows for the irregularity in whale song), *themes* are *stanzas* (tercets with exception of the last), and the *song* is a *poem* (7-20 minutes/lines in length).

UNITS	=	{A, B, C, D, E, F, G}
SUBPHRASES	=	{DE, FF}
PHRASES	=	{BC, DEDEFF, GGGGGG, AAAA}
THEMES	=	{BCBCBC, DEDEFFDEDEFF, GGGGGG, AAAA}
SONG	=	AAABCBCDEDEFFDEDEFFGGGGGGG
SONG SESSION	=	..A..BC..DEDEFF..G..A..BC..DEDEFF..G..
SOUND PATTERNS	=	{A, BC, DEDEFF, G}

Figure 1. Representation of the types of structural components typically present in sequences of sounds produced by singing humpback whales. Each letter represents one sound. Each individual sound is called a unit (different letters correspond to aurally distinctive sound units). Repeated groups of units are called phrases. Some phrases consist of repeated groups of subphrases. A theme is a set of repeated phrases. Songs consist of repeated theme sequences within a song session. We use the term 'sound pattern' to refer to any sound or set of sounds that is consistently repeated within a song session.

E. Mercado, et al.

Humpback song's rhyme sense leaves the listener in a place that is not sonically familiar to the song. In fact the "G" is a grand departure from the rest of the song—a kind of poetic anti-closural gesture that asks for response.

This long poem also uses passages (italicized) from: Whitehead, Hal, and Luke Rendell. *The Cultural Lives of Whales and Dolphins.* University of Chicago Press, 2014. *"That great god"* comes from W. S. Merwin's poem "For A Coming Extinction."

"Underwater Acoustics" was put to orchestration by George Lam at Chautauqua Institute 2018.

"Golden Record" uses lyrics from the actual Golden Record on the *Voyager* spacecraft launched in 1977. On this record scientists included (along with other songs) humpback whale song, as well as the composition "Jaat Kahan Ho" in Raga Bhairavi. The singer is Kesarbai Kerkar.

"Cultural Revolution": The last phrase *aa sakha, hamar sang bhajan baja* means *Come friend, play a song with me.*

"Interpreting Behaviors": The first couplet is a Hindi translation of two lines from Kimiko Hahn's poem "Ode to 52 Hz"; the original lines appear in italics at the end. "Ode to 52 Hz," from *Toxic Flora* by Kimiko Hahn. Copyright © 2010 by Kimiko Hahn. Used by permission of W. W. Norton & Company, Inc.

In "Sound Navigation and Ranging," "Sonar" uses words and phrases from: Alexander, Kristina. *Whales and Sonar: Environmental Exemptions for the Navy's Mid-Frequency Active Sonar Training*. Congressional Research Service, 2008. https://fas.org/sgp/crs/weapons/RL34403.pdf

The epigraph for this sequence is from "Praise Song for Oceania" in *Habitat Threshold*. Copyright © 2020 by Craig Santos Perez. Used by permission of Omnidawn Publishing. All rights reserved.

"RIMPAC" stands for "Rim of the Pacific," which is the largest world warfare exercise.

"Shift to Silence" takes words from the article: Sommer, Lauren. "Whales Get a Break as Pandemic Creates Quieter Oceans." *NPR*, NPR, 20 July 2020, https://www.npr.org/2020/07/20/891854646/whales-get-a-break-as-pandemic-creates-quieter-oceans.

"Why Whales Are Back in New York City" takes words from the article: Pierre-Louis, Kendra. "Why Whales Are Back in New York City." *Popular Science*, 26 Apr. 2021, https://www.popsci.com/new-york-city-whales/.

ACKNOWLEDGMENTS

Versions of the poems in this collection previously appear in:
    2River View, The Academy of American Poets Poem-a-Day, Arc Poetry, Asian American Literary Review, Cincinnati Review, The Collagist, diode, The DMQ Review, Ecotone, Guernica /A Magazine of Arts and Politics, Hawai'i Review, Kenyon Review, Killer Whale Journal, New England Review, Nimrod International Journal of Prose and Poetry, Orion, Pacific Review, Ploughshares, Poecology, Prairie Schooner, Quarterly West, and *Southern Humanities Review.*

Some have been anthologized in:
    Nepantla, An Anthology Dedicated to Queer Poets of Color, The Penguin Book of Indian Poets, Take A Stand: Art Against Hate, A Raven Chronicles Anthology, Literature & Composition: Reading, Writing, Thinking, and *The World I Leave You: Asian American Poets on Faith and Spirituality.*

Special thank you to the captains Cohen: Emily and Noel (and Ruby and Felix) for taking me on their vessel into the Santa Barbara Channel; and to the Hurley family: Ryan, Rachel, Lincoln, Sachi, and Katsu who gave me a place to stay in 'Ālewa Heights, opening their homes and hearts to me and these poems. The friendship and generosity of these two families is its own poetry.

Thanks to the whole Four Way Books team: Martha Rhodes, Ryan Murphy, Hannah Matheson, Sara Munjack, and Jonathan Blunk.

Thanks to my teachers and mentors: Craig Santos Perez and Allison Hedge Coke for their care. To Frank Stewart, Cynthia Franklin, Njoroge Njoroge, and to Subramanian Shankar. Thanks also to Chen Chen, Aimee Nezhukumatathil, and Craig Santos Perez for their words.

To Anjani Prashad for the use of her painting "Ventral Pleats" for the cover of this book.

Special thanks to Emerson College's Faculty Advancement Fund Grant for helping in the completion of this book.

To my beloveds who offered me support and community, a heart full of gratitude. Thanks to my family including Kajal Sahmi and Enkidu Shehrni. And to Jordan Andrew Miles who met me when these poems met me.

Thanks to: Charmila Ajmera, Kazim Ali, Hari Alluri, Mohamed Q. Amin, Zaman Amin, Ryan Artes, Andre Bagoo, Anna Lena Phillips Bell, Liz Bradfield, Mary Kovaleski Byrnes, Amalia Bueno, Nicole Cooley, Will Depoo, Will Nu'utupu Giles, Joanna Gordon, Andil Gosine, Jaimie Gusman, Kimiko Hahn, Joseph Han, Corinne and Jon Hyde, Liz Jaikaran, Roy Kamada, Lee Kava, Bryan Kamaoli Kuwada, Devi Laskar, Uly Loken, Shikha Saklani Malaviya, Nadia Misir, Joce Ng, Shivanee Ramlochan, Anna V. Q. Ross, No'u Revilla, Anjoli Roy, Milton Sakuoka, Chandanie Somwaru, Lyz Soto, Sophia Strid, Adeeba Shahid Taluker, Novuyo Rosa Tshuma, Rushi Vyas, Katie Williams, and Aiko Yamashiro.

This book began on the US-occupied Kingdom of Hawaiʻi, the traditional ʻāina of the Kanaka ʻŌiwi who still practice aloha ʻāina despite American militarism, settler colonial and American genocidal legislation.

Illegally overthrown in 1893 with the imprisonment of Queen Liliʻuokalani, the constitutional monarchy was replaced by a military government who served the white, American capitalists that sought to drain Hawaiʻi of its resources. The People, despite occupation, practice radical acts of sovereignty.

I wrote beneath the gaze of Lēʻahi, in the sprinkling of gentle rains in Mānoa, under the eye of Makapuʻu, and in the surf of Kaʻena. I am grateful for the kai, the ʻāina, and the People whom I met there, who showed me the limits of my American poetry, and mirrored for me a practice of kuleana to our stories and to community.

In acknowledgement of this history, and my representing the American government as a graduate student of the University of Hawaiʻi, Mānoa, who enacted colonial violence in their attempted construction of the Thirty Meter Telescope without going through the People's channels and protocols, I acknowledge my complicity in the settler colonial project and seek to amplify the work of Kanaka Maoli poets and writers who resisted, who are resisting, and who will continue to resist.

In this spirit I offer this song of praise and vandana:

IN PRAISE OF HAWAI'I

From Lē'ahi's emerald crater
to Mauna a Wākea's spout of 'i'iwi's
        crimson feathers, the glory

of Her Majesty Lili'uokalani billows
        from summits and pyroclastic flow,
land still forged in the core

        where 'Ōiwi resist in dance, in kalo
lo'i, sovereign hearts crowned in
        the verdant halo of Mount Ka'ala.

Ham samundar se toke dekh sakeli,
        aapan anubandhan se mukt bhaili.
Parnaam, hath jordke. *Namastasyai.*

        Namastasyai. Namastasyai namo namah.

ABOUT THE AUTHOR

RAJIV MOHABIR is the author of *The Taxidermist's Cut* (2014 Intro to Poetry Prize, Four Way Books 2016), *The Cowherd's Son* (2015 Kundiman Prize, Tupelo Press 2017), and *Cutlish* (Four Way Books 2021), which was awarded the Eric Hoffer Medal Provocateur, second place in the 2022 Guyana Prize for Literature, was longlisted for the 2022 PEN/Voelcker Prize, and was a finalist for both the New England Book Award and the National Book Critics Circle Award. His memoir, *Antiman: A Hybrid Memoir* (Restless Books 2021), won the Forward Indies Award for LGBTQ+ Nonfiction and was a finalist for the 2022 PEN/America Open Book Award, 2021 Randy Shilts Award for Gay Nonfiction, and 2021 Lambda Literary Award for Gay Memoir/Biography. As a translator, his version of *I Even Regret Night: Holi Songs of Demerara* (Kaya 2019) won the Harold Morton Landon Translation Award from the Academy of American Poets in 2020. In 2022, he was awarded a Massachusetts Cultural Council Fellowship. He teaches in the MFA program at the University of Colorado Boulder.

PUBLICATION OF THIS BOOK WAS MADE POSSIBLE
BY GRANTS AND DONATIONS. WE ARE ALSO GRATEFUL
TO THOSE INDIVIDUALS WHO PARTICIPATED IN
OUR BUILD A BOOK PROGRAM. THEY ARE:

Anonymous (14), Robert Abrams, Michael Ansara, Kathy Aponick, Jean
Ball, Sally Ball, Clayre Benzadon, Adrian Blevins, Laurel Blossom, Adam
Bohannon, Betsy Bonner, Patricia Bottomley, Lee Briccetti, Joel Brouwer,
Susan Buttenwieser, Anthony Cappo, Paul and Brandy Carlson, Dan
Clarke, Mark Conway, Elinor Cramer, Kwame Dawes, Michael Anna de
Armas, John Del Peschio, Brian Komei Dempster, Rosalynde Vas Dias,
Patrick Donnelly, Lynn Emanuel, Blas Falconer, Jennifer Franklin, John
Gallaher, Reginald Gibbons, Rebecca Kaiser Gibson, Dorothy Tapper
Goldman, Julia Guez, Naomi Guttman and Jonathan Mead, Forrest
Hamer, Luke Hankins, Yona Harvey, KT Herr, Karen Hildebrand, Carlie
Hoffman, Glenna Horton, Thomas and Autumn Howard, Catherine
Hoyser, Elizabeth Jackson, Linda Susan Jackson, Jessica Jacobs and
Nickole Brown, Lee Jenkins, Elizabeth Kanell, Nancy Kassell, Maeve
Kinkead, Victoria Korth, Brett Lauer and Gretchen Scott, Howard
Levy, Owen Lewis and Susan Ennis, Margaree Little, Sara London and
Dean Albarelli, Tariq Luthun, Myra Malkin, Louise Mathias, Victoria
McCoy, Lupe Mendez, Michael and Nancy Murphy, Kimberly Nunes,
Susan Okie and Walter Weiss, Cathy McArthur Palermo, Veronica
Patterson, Jill Pearlman, Marcia and Chris Pelletiere, Sam Perkins, Susan
Peters and Morgan Driscoll, Maya Pindyck, Megan Pinto, Kevin Prufer,
Martha Rhodes and Jean Brunel, Paula Rhodes, Louise Riemer, Peter
and Jill Schireson, Rob Schlegel, Yoana Setzer, Soraya Shalforoosh,
Mary Slechta, Diane Souvaine, Barbara Spark, Catherine Stearns, Jacob
Strautmann, Yerra Sugarman, Arthur Sze and Carol Moldaw, Marjorie
and Lew Tesser, Dorothy Thomas, Rushi Vyas, Martha Webster and
Robert Fuentes, Rachel Weintraub and Allston James, Abby Wender and
Rohan Weerasinghe, and Monica Youn.